Surviving

Financial Crisis

by Loren Lumpe and Ray Mirly

SAINT LOUIS

Thomas J. Doyle, Editor

Your comments and suggestions concerning this material are solicited. Please write to Product Manager, Youth and Adult Bible Studies, Concordia Publishing House, 3558 South Jefferson Ave., St. Louis, MO 63118-3968.

Copyright © 1996 Concordia Publishing House
3558 S. Jefferson Avenue, St. Louis, MO 63118-3968
Manufactured in the United States of America

1 2 3 4 5 6 7 8 9 10   05 04 03 02 01 00 99 98 97 96

Contents

How Does One Get into a Financial Crisis?

Focusing Our Sights

It is probably safe to say that no one purposely tries to have a financial crisis. In this session we will explore how a financial crisis often develops. We will discuss our views concerning money and wealth. We will learn what God says about money. We will learn how Satan, the world, and our own sinful self tempt us to make unwise choices with our use of money. We will also learn that Jesus Christ forgives us for our mismanagement of resources that He has provided and offers His help and guidance in any situation, including a financial crisis.

Focusing Our Attention

Put an "A" in front of the statement if you agree with it and a "D" if you disagree.

____Money is the measure of success.

____Money can solve most problems.

____Money is the key to survival in this dog-eat-dog world.

____Power is in the holder of the purse strings.

____Money in the bank means security.

After you have completed this exercise individually, discuss your agreement or disagreement for each with the group. See if you can reach consensus as a group as to whether you agree or disagree with the statements.

(Adapted from *Opposites Attract: Turning Differences into Opportunities* by Jack and Carole Myhall. Copyright 1990 by Jack and Carole Mayhall. NavPress, Colorado Springs, Colorado.)

Try this exercise: Stare at this word for 60 seconds: *Money*. Now write the words that come to mind. Then circle the additional words from the following list that you think of when you consider money.

envy	lust	fulfillment	happiness
fear	scorn	useful	shopping
guilt	power	leisure	social status
dreams	goals	responsibility	freedom
status	fun	serious	worry
security	joy	give	love
temptation	control	hope	

The words you choose may be a clue to what money means to you and may help you untangle your own attitudes about it. As a group discuss the attitudes toward money that the words you circled or listed reflect.

Focusing on the Issue

"It seemed so easy," said Becky. "The salesman said that we could make the purchase on the installment plan. You know, $50 down and $50 every month. Joe and I had always talked about making a budget, but we never did."

The credit card bill was larger than Becky expected. There wasn't enough money to go around. She paid the minimum payment. During the next month Emily, her daughter, needed new shoes for school. She did not have money in the checking account nor enough cash, so she charged them. The refrigerator stopped working during the same month. Of course the repair person had to be paid. The only way Becky could fix the refrigerator was to use her credit card.

When the next month's credit card bill arrived, Becky gasped in disbelief. The balance was higher than the month before. The minimum payment was higher as well. She barely was able to make the minimum payment. She vowed she would not use the credit card during the next month.

Becky knew she shouldn't use the credit card until the balance could be paid down. The car quit in the middle of rush hour. The tow truck driver demanded to be paid before he would move her car. The police demanded that the car be moved immediately. What was she to do? She had to use the credit card. She did not have another way to pay the tow truck driver.

Finally, the next credit card bill arrived. When it did, Becky's concern was justified. The minimum payment was greater than the amount of money she had … what was she to do?

The Cost of Credit

Outstanding Balance	$ 2,000
Interest Rate	18.5%
Minimum Payment	2.8%*
Interest Cost over the Loan Period	$ 1,906
Payoff Period	Over 11 years

* or $20.00, whichever is greater

7

Insights about Crisis

1. Define the word *crisis:*

Share your definition with your study partners.

2. As a group, brainstorm what causes a crisis. You can use Becky's situation or your own experiences.

3. What emotions do you believe Becky experienced when the last credit card bill arrived?

Focusing on God's Word

In the Holy Scriptures, there are numerous references to money, wealth, and possessions. Often times, what the Bible says is misquoted. For example, you have probably heard someone insist that the Scriptures say that "money is the root of all evil." What 1 Timothy 6:10 actually says is, "For the *love* of money is a root of all kinds of evil."

❖

The devil's goal, through his temptations, is to undermine our faith and trust in God. He knows that money is necessary for everything from life's basics to luxuries. He wants to turn our heart away from dependence upon God. He strives to plant in us doubts about meeting daily financial needs. He wants us to worry about our lack of wealth or possessions. Satan, the world, and our own sinful self tempt us to misuse the gifts God has given us, including our money.

The following Bible passages and questions will help you to better understand how Satan, the world, and our sinful self can tempt us to mismanage money leading us into a financial crisis.

1. It is embarrassing to live in the most comfortable time in history and be unhappy. Discuss this statement based upon the words of Matthew 6:24 and Philippians 4:6–7.

2. Read Matthew 6:19–21. Discuss how our "inner desires" ("out of the heart") lead us into unwise decisions.

❖

3. What are the key points made in James 1:13–15? How do these relate to unwise uses of money?

4. Jesus prepared the Twelve for their life of discipleship. Matthew 16:21–28 records Jesus' efforts to prepare the disciples for His death. Within His discourse, He issued a warning in verses 24–26.

a. What is Jesus' warning to His disciples?

b. What is the potential, ultimate, outcome of desiring the "world"?

5. What does God promise to us through Christ when we confess our sinful use of money? See 1 John 1:9.

❖

6. As those for whom Christ died, why is it imperative to keep our hearts and minds focused upon Him when going through financial crises? Read Romans 7:22–25 to help you.

Focusing on My Life

1. Take several minutes to reflect upon how you have viewed and used money. If you are currently facing a financial crisis, how have your views and use of money contributed to it? If not, how could your views and use lead to a financial crisis?

2. Brainstorm as a group an answer to the following question, "Why has God given you money and how does He want you to use it?"

3. Describe to a partner how God's forgiveness in Christ for the misuse of the resources He has given to you provides you new hope as you face the days ahead. Read to each other the invitation Jesus provides to all sinners in Matthew 11:28–30.

To Close

Sing or speak stanzas 1 and 4 of the hymn "Take My Life, O Lord, Renew."

Take my life, O Lord, renew,
Consecrate my heart to You;
Take my moments and my days;
Let them sing Your ceaseless praise.

❖

Take my silver and my gold,
All is Yours a thousandfold;
Take my intellect, and use
Ev'ry pow'r as You shall choose.

Focusing on the Week Ahead

Review how you (your family) have been
using the financial resources God has given
you. Think together (individually) how you can
better use these resources. Take your needs to
God in prayer.

How Does One Cope with a Financial Crisis?

2

Focusing Our Sights

In this session we will concentrate on discovering the resources that God has given Christians to deal with crises. These resources certainly are applicable to how He would have us deal with a financial crisis. We will search the Scriptures to see how a young man's foolishness led to a financial crisis. We will also learn from the Scriptures about how God's grace works even in the lives of those who have foolishly mismanaged that which He had given. Through the study of a real life crisis insights will be gained for real life answers.

Focusing Our Attention

1. I am able to talk with _____ about my thoughts, experiences, and desires.
2. I am aware of my feelings and am willing to share them with _____.
3. I am _____ with making decisions.
4. I am _____ with my income and spending practices.
5. I handle failure in a _____ manner.

Focusing on the Issue

Discuss the following saying, "If God seems far away, guess who moved?"

Financial crisis is often accompanied by feelings of being alone or helpless. Those who are in crisis frequently are embarrassed. They find it difficult to believe that they were unable to control their spending habits. Others have low self-esteem. They find it hard to admit that they have failed even though they expect to fail. The crisis deepens because they refuse to admit they are in a "financial mess."

1. Why would God seem far away to one who is in a financial crisis?

2. Why would someone in a financial crisis be unwilling (unable) to reveal the problem to a fellow Christian?

3. What feelings would a Christian most likely have to cope with when facing a financial crisis?

❖

4. What temptations would confront one who experiences a financial crisis?

Focusing on God's Word

A financial crisis may occur through no apparent misuse of God-given resources. Or it may be created by inappropriate use of God's gifts. No matter what the reason for the crisis, the Parable of the Lost Son, Luke 15:11–24 has much to say to anyone experiencing such a crisis.

1. What word in this parable best describes the cause of the young son's crisis?

Explain how this word might apply to your financial crisis or the crisis a friend or loved one is experiencing.

2. Why does the Lord permit us to "hit bottom" before we come to our senses? See Luke 11:14–17.

3. How far away does God place Himself from us and our problems? See Matthew 28:20b; Psalm 23; Psalm 46; and/or John 10.

4. What do we learn about God's love for us, even when we have "squandered" everything?

5. Does God "restore" everything we lose due to mismanagement of money? Discuss.

Focusing on My Life

From the following list, select *five* items that best describe what you prize most for your life.

Peace

Love

Good social life

Peer affirmation

Family

Comfortable life

Positive self-image

Adventure

Security

Eternal life

Close friendship

Forgiveness

Sense of fulfillment

Closeness with God

Freedom

1. Upon further reflection upon the parable of the Prodigal Son, what five choices from the above list do you believe he would have made before he left home? during his crisis? after his return home? Compare the prodigal son's possible choices to your own life?

2. How many of your choices require possession of money? Why would this be true?

3. How many of your choices have at least the potential to affect your use of money?

❖

4. Share with the group your reason(s) for the choices you made.

5. What does your relationship with your heavenly Father give you that no money can buy? Review the passages suggested in number 3 of "Focusing on God's Word."

To Close

Sing or speak together stanzas 1–2 of "Lord, Take My Hand and Lead Me."

Lord, take my hand and lead me
    Upon life's way;
Direct, protect, and feed me
    From day to day.
Without Your grace and favor
    I go astray;
So take my hand, O Savior,
    And lead the way.

Lord, when the tempest rages,
    I need not fear;
For You, the Rock of Ages,
    Are always near.
Close by Your side abiding,
    I fear no foe,
For when Your hand is guiding,
    In peace I go.

Focusing on the Week Ahead

1. Use one or both of the stanzas of "Lord, Take My Hand and Lead Me" as your daily prayer.

2. Write your own prayer incorporating in your thoughts those things for which you have learned in this lesson you most need the Lord's help.

3. Read Psalm 46. Meditate especially upon verses 1 and 10.

Credit Card
A means for buying something you don't need, at a price you can't afford, with money you don't have.

❖

3

After the Crisis— Where Do We Go from Here?

Focusing Our Sights

When a storm passes, the natural reaction is to breathe a sigh of relief and relax. One might want to do the same after experiencing a financial crisis. Instead, it is important once the crisis has passed to develop a plan. In this lesson the focus will be on charting a course for the future. You will study in God's Word about prudent management. You will be challenged, with God's help, to develop a personal financial plan.

Focusing Our Attention

Before one can understand a sentence, paragraph, or book, one must understand the words. Within a group of five people you might have five different definitions for the same word. Write your definition for each of the following words. Compare your definition with that of the group. Try to develop a consensus definition for each word.

Faithful:_____

Selfish: _____

Abundance: _____

Accumulate: _____

Steward: _____

Prudent: _____

Focusing on the Issue

1. Review in your mind what caused you or someone you love to have a financial crisis. You may want to review sessions 1 and 2. Share in a general way with the group one or two contributing factors. Try to discover factors that are common to many in the group and those which are unique.

2. What does it mean to be prudent? What does prudence have to do with the control of one's life choices? Read Proverbs 1:3; 13:16; 14:15; and 22:3.

3. What does it mean to be faithful in the use of money and wealth?

4. What changes must you make to avoid a future financial crisis? The group should work together to develop a general list of goals. Privately add goals that are unique to your situation.

5. The following is a list of helps that are available to all Christians. Discuss as a group how each one of the following can be of help in developing financial control?

Bible study

Worship

Holy Communion

Prayer

Church community

Focusing on God's Word

1. Study together the following sections of Holy Scripture. In each parable what determined whether the person was wise or foolish, faithful or unfaithful, prudent or imprudent.

Luke 12:13–21

Luke 12:22–33

Luke 12:42–48

2. Jesus frequently spoke about management decisions. In the following parables poor decisions were made. What was the root problem in each parable? Which of the parables teach about prudence?
Luke 12:16–21

Matthew 25:1–13

Matthew 7:26–27

3. John 12:1–8 records another example of the use of God's gifts. Judas and Jesus had different opinions concerning Mary's use of some expensive perfume. How do Jesus' words apply to you today?

4. Read the parable of the talents, Matthew 25:14–30. What made the two servants "good" in the master's judgment?

What caused the master to reject the management of the one talent?

What is the point of this parable?

Focusing on My Life

God has entrusted you with the responsibility to manage a certain amount of talents. As a group, discuss how the words *faithful* and *prudent* apply to Christian management of one's talents. After discussing this, write a short paragraph that expresses your understanding how you can be faithful and prudent in managing that which God has given you.

At times we may mismanage those gifts God has graciously given to us. We will be neither *faithful* nor *prudent*. At those times we look to the cross where Jesus suffered and died for our sins. At the cross we find complete forgiveness for our sinful thoughts, words, and actions. At the cross we find the power to transform our sinful ways—including the ways in which we misuse the limited resources God has provided to us. Jesus' love for us motivates us to use our money in ways that will glorify God and enables us to make wise choices.

A Christian's Four Basic Uses for Money

For family	but not to "spoil" them
For retirement	but not in excess
To enjoy the fruits of our labor	but not overdone
To carry out the Lord's work	cannot be overdone

Discuss as a group the Christian's four basic uses for money described in the chart. Do you agree or disagree? Why?

To Close

Speak or sing together stanzas 2 and 5 of "Take My Life, O Lord, Renew."

Take my hands and let them do
Works that show my love for You;
Take my feet and lead their way,
Never let them go astray.

❖

Make my will Your holy shrine,
It shall be no longer mine.
Take my heart, it is Your own;
It shall be Your royal throne.

Focusing on the Week Ahead

Throughout this week meditate daily upon the following two Bible passages, "No servant can serve two masters. Either he will hate the one and love the other, or he will be devoted to the one and despise the other. You cannot serve both God and Money" (Luke 16:13); and "… as for me and my household, we will serve the LORD" (Joshua 24:15).

❖

Develop a Personal (Household) Budget

In order to develop a budget you must first determine your regular income (weekly, bi-weekly, monthly) and a list of expenses. Use the following example or develop your own.

	Week 1	Week 2	Week 3	Week 4
1. Husband's gross income	_____	_____	_____	_____
2. Wife's gross income	_____	_____	_____	_____
3. Additional income	_____	_____	_____	_____
Total income	_____	_____	_____	_____

If you are paid weekly, total the four weeks together to arrive at a monthly income. If you are paid bi-weekly add the two pay periods for the month together to determine your monthly income. If your income varies from month to month, estimate what your lowest month's income for the last 12 months and use that number.

Total monthly personal
(household) income _____

Next you must determine your monthly expenses. Fill in the blanks with your actual expense for each item. You may need to add items. Not all items will apply to you. Simply put a zero in items that do not apply.

1. Church offering _____

2. Mortgage/Rent _____

3. Electric _____

4. Gas _____

5. Phone _____

6. Garbage _____

7. Water _____

8. Groceries _____

9. Eating out _____

10. Car payment(s) _____

11. Car insurance _____

12. Car repairs _____

13. Gasoline/Oil _____

14. Clothing _____

15. Child care _____

16. Entertainment _____

17. Life insurance _____

18. Home insurance _____

19. Credit cards _____

20. Health care _____

21. Subscriptions _____

22. Savings _____

23. Investments _____

❖

24. Retirement _____

25. Taxes (Includes real estate
    and personal property)_____

26. Mad Money _____

27. _____

28. _____

29. _____

30. _____

Total Monthly Expenses _____

Expenses must not exceed income. If they do, you must reduce your spending until your expenses balance with your income. You cannot manage your money prudently or faithfully if you do not follow this simple, but important rule.

Cash Flow Traps

As you analyze your cash flow, watch out for some of the cash flow traps.

Installment Debt. Installment debt is incurred whenever you decide to pay for an item "over time." Americans hold over one billion credit cards. And they're becoming a serious problem for many people.

The "Buying-up" Problem. Some people find it difficult to save because they are always increasing their debt whenever their income increases. They trade up to a more expensive house or car as soon as they are able to afford the monthly payments. We call this the "buying-up" problem.

Non-Monthly Periodic Expenses. Non-monthly periodic expenses can take you by surprise and force you to spend money you hadn't anticipated. These "pop-up" bills, such as automobile insurance or property taxes, can take a real bite out of your cash flow.

Invisible Commitment. Some purchases carry a built-in invisible commitment. For example, buying a new home also includes upkeep expenses such as the lawn, trees, a garage door opener, new furniture, drapes, and on and on. Be sure you examine this invisible commitment whenever you make a purchase.

Tracking Monthly Cash Flow

It is essential for good money management to keep track of cash flow (place, date, and amount spent, and what was purchased). The following is a simple method for keeping track of your cash flow. If you have a home computer, simple home financial management programs are available at a reasonable cost.

Monthly Cash Flow   Month_____

Contributions	Groceries	Electric _____(Amt.)
Where/Date/Amt.	Where/Date/Amt.	Gas _____(Amt.)

		Phone _____(Amt.)
_____	_____	Garbage _____(Amt.)
_____	_____	Water _____(Amt.)
_____	_____	Mortgage/Rent _____(Amt.)
Total _____	Total _____	Car pay. _____ (Amt.)

Eating out   **Car repairs**   Car ins. _____ (Amt.)

Where/Date/Amt.   Where/Date/Amt.   Life ins. _____ (Amt.)

_____	_____	Home ins. _____ (Amt.)
_____	_____	Credit card _____ (Amt.)
_____	_____	Savings _____ (Amt.)
_____	Total _____	Taxes _____ (Amt.)
_____		Investments _____ (Amt.)

Total _____   **Miscellaneous**

Where/Date/Amt.   **Child care**

Gasoline/Oil   _____   Where/Date/Amt.

Where/Date/Amt.

_____	_____	_____
_____	_____	_____
_____	_____	_____
_____	_____	_____
_____	Total_____	_____
_____	_____	

Total_____   _____   Total _____

Entertainment

Clothing   Where/Date/Amt.   **Subscriptions**

Where/Date/Amt.   _____   Where/Date/Amt.

_____	_____	_____
_____	_____	_____
_____	_____	_____
Total_____	Total_____	Total _____

Add all of the totals _____
This number should not exceed your monthly income.

❖

Showing Love to One Another

Focusing Our Sights

The parable of the Prodigal Son was the focus of session 2. His father anxiously waited for him to come to his senses. He welcomed him home with open arms and restored him to his place in the family. The focus of this lesson will be on God's grace toward us. You will also be encouraged in turn to share God's love with those you know who are in crisis. St. John urges us to "love one another" (1 John 3:11). He tells us, "This is how we know what love is: Jesus Christ laid down his life for us. And we ought to lay down our lives for our brothers" (1 John 3:16). As we have experienced God's unconditional, forgiving love, so we are compelled to share it with those burdened with guilt and despair.

Focusing Our Attention

Human nature is selfish. The self-centered person focuses upon personal needs. Even Christians fail to look beyond self. We Christians, however, only need read Philippians 2 to be reminded how Jesus "humbled Himself." He traded heaven for a cross. In his teaching, Jesus emphasized the concern that believers should have for others.

Discuss the following statements. Perhaps you can add to these often heard comments.

"The poor have only themselves to blame. If they were more industrious they could help themselves to end their poverty."

"If they had not spent all their money on foolish things, they would not be in the trouble they are in today. Since they got themselves into trouble, let them get themselves out of it."

"He who makes his bed must sleep in it."

Focusing on the Issue

1. In what ways have you been helped by others?

2. In what ways have others made your crisis more difficult?

3. Develop a list of suggestions, based upon your experiences, that this group can offer to those who are involved in a financial crisis.

❖

4. How might you be able to help another person who is experiencing a financial crisis?

5. What spiritual resources have been most helpful to you during the time of financial crisis? How would they be of importance to another person going through a similar crisis?

Focusing on God's Word

It is easy to think that when one has been in a financial crisis that there is no way he can help another person in financial crisis. This feeling comes partly from a lack of self-confidence. It can also be caused by unresolved guilt. This is not the message of the Holy Scriptures. In God's Law we are told that we are to "love our neighbor as ourselves."

1. Of what fact does St. John remind each of us in 1 John 3:1? Compare John 3:16 with this fact.

2. What is the message of 1 John 3:10?

3. Luke 10:30–36 records the parable of the good Samaritan. How does this parable apply to our understanding of the Christian's response to a person in need?

4. Psalm 23 and John 10 give us great understanding regarding the relationship Jesus Christ has established with us. What help is found in these two sections of Scripture for us when we face a crisis? What help can we give to others by sharing these sections with others who are in crisis?

Focusing on My Life

Martin Luther gave us a beautiful explanation regarding what our heavenly Father does for us. He wrote: "I believe that God has made me and all creatures; that He has given me my body and soul, eyes, ears, and all my

35

❖

members, my reason and all my senses, and still takes care of them.

He also gives me clothing and shoes, food and drink, house and home, wife and children, land, animals, and all I have. He richly and daily provides me with all that I need to support this body and life.

He defends me against all danger and guards and protects me from all evil.

All this He does only out of fatherly, divine goodness and mercy, without any merit or worthiness in me. For all this it is my duty to thank and praise, serve and obey Him.

This is most certainly true."

Luther's Small Catechism copyright © 1986 CPH.

Every time you begin to worry about your earthly life, review these words.

To Close

Speak or sing stanza 6 of "Take My Life, O Lord, Renew."
Take my love; my Lord, I pour
At Your feet its treasure store;
Take my self, Lord, let me be
Yours alone eternally.

Focusing on the Weeks Ahead

Search the Scriptures daily.
Be a person of prayer.
Worship regularly.
Attend the Lord's Supper frequently.
Ask the Lord to enable you to be prudent and faithful.
To God be the glory!

Appendix

Consumer Credit Counseling Service

If you are having difficulty in paying your credit obligations, you can call Consumer Credit **Counseling Service**—a non-profit counseling service at 1-800-9NO-DEBT.

Check Your Credit Report

You can obtain a free copy of your credit report by writing to TRW. Your request must include the following:

- Your full name (including middle initial and generation such as Jr.)
- Your address (and previous addresses for the past five years)
- Your Social Security number
- Your birth date
- Your spouse's first name, if you're married
- A photocopy of your driver's license or a copy of a current utility or phone bill for verification of your identity and address.
- Your signature
  Mail the information to:
  TRW Consumer Assistance
  P.O. Box 2350
  Chatsworth, CA 91313-2350

❖

TRW will issue a free report once a year. If you want more than one report in a calendar year, you can purchase a second one for a fee of $8.00. This request should be sent to: TRW; P.O. Box 2104; Allen, TX 75013-2104. By law, credit agencies must send you a complimentary report if you have been denied credit within the past 30 days.

Whoever loves money never has money enough; whoever loves wealth is never satisfied with his income. (Ecclesiastes 5:10)

Leaders Notes

Session 1

How Does One Get into a Financial Crisis?

❖ Focusing Our Sights

(About 1 minute.)
Read aloud.

❖ Focusing Our Attention

(About 10 minutes.)
Ask participants to put an "A" in front of each statement in which they are in agreement and a "D" if they disagree with it. After all the participants have completed the exercise, as a group try to reach a consensus answer for each statement.

Or ...

Complete the second suggested activity. If your group meets longer than one hour, you may wish to do both activities.

❖ Focusing on the Issue

(About 10 minutes.)
Read the story about Becky's financial crisis. Ask the following question, "Can anyone identify with Becky's problem?" Discuss with the group the question: "What caused Becky's financial crisis?" Ask if there are any reactions to "The Cost of

Credit" at the end of this section. Finally, discuss the three questions in the section "Insights about Crisis." Answers will vary.

❖ Focusing on God's Word

(About 15 minutes.)

Read the three opening paragraphs as a way of introducing the Bible study. Have a member of the group read aloud the suggested Bible passages before answering each question.

1. Many put an improper value upon money (wealth). These two passages address the issue of faith. In whom or in what do we put our trust? St. Paul reminds us to put our trust in our heavenly Father.

2. For a greater understanding of Matthew 6:19–21 see Luke 12:16–21. The riches of the farmer had no bearing upon the length of his life. It certainly had no benefit for his eternal life. Jesus warns about putting our faith in earthly treasures.

3. There are usually three stages to temptation: desire, sin, and death. If time allows, review Genesis 3:1–7 where Satan played upon Eve's sense of sight and desire for something good to lead her to disobey God.

4. (a) Jesus warned his disciples that the soul is far more valuable than one's body (earthly life). Discipleship will at times demand self-denial. The faith of the Christian is such that to serve Christ is of first importance. When we place anything above God in our lives, we break the First Commandment, "You shall have no other gods." (b) Jesus clearly told the disciples that the world only has everlasting death to offer ("forfeits his soul").

5. God promises full and complete forgiveness through faith in Christ Jesus to repentant sinners.

6. The name Jesus means "He will save His people" (Matt. 1:21). St. Paul reminds us in Romans 7:22–25 that the "Old Adam" that is within each of us will lead us to sin. To follow the Old Adam causes "wretchedness." "Who will rescue me from this body of death? Thanks be to God—through

Jesus Christ our Lord!" The point is that only through faith in Jesus Christ are we victorious over sin, death, and the devil. Only Jesus can rescue us from sin and its devastating effects on our lives.

❖ Focusing on My Life

(About 12 minutes.)

Give the participants about two to three minutes to work individually on question 1. Remind them to think about the points brought out in the Bible study.

2. Brainstorm with the group why God has given us money and how He wants us to use it.

3. Allow time for volunteers to share the hope God had, does, and will provide them through faith in Jesus.

❖ To Close

(About 3 minutes.)

Sing or speak the stanzas of the hymn "Take My Life, O Lord, Renew" as printed in the study guide. Allow participants to share prayer needs with the entire group or with a partner. Have volunteers pray for the identified needs.

❖ Focusing on the Week Ahead

Read the instructions found in this section. Encourage everyone to take time during the week to meditate upon the Bible study from this session. Urge them to use the message of the Bible study to focus upon their own use of their God-given resources. Remind them that God does answer prayer.

❖

Session 2

How Does One Cope with a Financial Crisis?

❖ Focusing Our Sights

(About 1 minute.)
Read aloud and discuss the goals for this session.

❖ Focusing Our Attention

(About 5 minutes.)
Permit participants time to fill in the blanks. Numbers three and four may cause some difficulty. Words such as "comfortable or uncomfortable" would be appropriate. Discuss each of these statements as a group. The idea is to break the ice so that all the participants will freely share their thoughts and feelings.

❖ Focusing on the Issue

(About 10 minutes.)
Open this section by discussing the question "If God seems far away, guess who moved?" If necessary, share with the group Christ's promise of Matthew 28:20 or Matthew 11:28. After completing the discussion read the paragraph regarding the feelings that accompany financial crisis. Then discuss the four questions. Answers will vary.

44

❖ Focusing on God's Word

(About 15 minutes.)

Read the introductory paragraph to the Bible study. Then read as a group Luke 15:11–24. Discuss the feelings that the group has regarding the lost son. Also discuss why they have these feelings.

1. The word that best describes the action of the young man that led to his crisis is "squandered." Discuss as a group just what this word means. Discuss the meaning of this word from the context of what the young man did with his inheritance. Squandered is a strong word. Perhaps no one in your group feels they have squandered their money, but ask them if they have used it "inappropriately" or "unwisely." Is there a difference between what the young man did and they themselves? In what way?

2. Ask the participants: "If the young man had not run out of money, how would the parable end?" Throughout history God has permitted us to use our free will—a free will tainted by sin. Sinners are very good at rationalizing their actions or making excuses. We must feel the full judgment of God's law and all of the accompanying negative consequences before we recognize that we have sinned. At times, God must let us feel the fire of hell lapping at our bodies before we admit our sin, repent, and ask for forgiveness.

3. Draw upon the discussion from the last section to discuss the point that God never leaves us. Read as a group Psalm 23, Psalm 46, or John 10 if you have time. This Word of God assures us that God is with us in good times and bad.

4. In this question it is imperative that you apply the Gospel to today's discussion. Sins great and small are all wiped away by Christ's life, death, and resurrection. Read and discuss as a group 1 John 2:1–2 which clearly says that Christ's blood cleanses us of our sins. Do not let anyone leave your class today believing that their sins are too great for God to forgive.

5. YES! If, not in this life, then certainly in the life to

come. Indeed, if we go bankrupt or contract an incurable illness, God may not restore us to our prebankrupt or pre-health-crisis condition. It is important to have the group read Romans 8:28, 31–39 and 1 Corinthians 10:13. God never gives us more than we can endure. Psalm 23:5 assures us that He will "prepare a table before us" even in the face of our enemies.

❖ Focusing on My Life

(About 15 minutes.)

Have members of the group do the exercise individually. Allow no more than 3–5 minutes. Have each participant answer question 1. After two minutes ask them to share their answers. Try to arrive at a group consensus. Have each person answer questions 2 and 3 individually. Encourage class members to share their choices and reasons (number 4). Discuss question 5 with the group.

If time permits, discuss the definition for a credit card found at the end of this lesson.

❖ To Close

(About 5 minutes.)

Sing or speak together the hymn as printed in the study guide. Have members of the class share concerns that are currently weighing upon their hearts. Invite volunteers to take these concerns to the Lord in prayer.

❖ Focusing on the Week Ahead

(About 3 minutes.)

Go through the assignment for the week. Encourage everyone to write their prayer and to add to it as the week progresses. Suggest that they read Psalm 46 daily, meditating upon a different verse each day.

Session 3

After the Crisis—
Where Do We Go from Here?

❖ Focusing Our Sights

(About 1 minute.)
Read aloud and discuss briefly the goals for this session.

❖ Focusing Our Attention

(About 7 minutes.)
Read the opening paragraph of this section. Have each participant write a brief definition for the six words. Appoint someone to be secretary so that the group can compile their definitions until they arrive at a common understanding of each word. This will be important later in the lesson.

❖ Focusing on the Issue

(About 15 minutes.)
Have each person answer question 1 individually. After about 1–2 minutes, have the group try to discover factors that contributed to their (or someone that they know) financial crisis which are common to the group and those which are unique.

2. Have the group read and discuss Proverbs 1:3; 13:16; 14:15; 22:3. Then answer question 2.

3. Discuss this question in the context of a bank teller

and a cashier. Apply this discussion to the people in the group.

4. Be sure to encourage each person to add their personal goal(s) to the group list.

5. The Holy Spirit works through the means of grace (Word and Sacrament) to bring us to faith and to keep us in the true faith to life everlasting. The emphasis of this discussion is to remind each participant that during a crisis because of shame, guilt, or other human emotions and feelings, we often stay away from church, Bible class, and the Lord's Supper. Especially during a crisis, a Christian needs to partake of the means of grace, pray, and remain in fellowship with his or her fellow Christians.

❖ Focusing on God's Word

(About 15 minutes.)

1. Jesus taught by means of parables. The three suggested Scripture readings are parables of Jesus. A parable is commonly defined as an earthly story with a heavenly or spiritual meaning. In verses 13–21, Jesus' point is that the rich man's faith was in the things of this world. His obvious problem was one of greed. He did not have an eternal focus. In verses 22–33, Jesus clearly teaches that our heavenly Father will give us everything that we need for this life and especially for our eternal life. His point is that the spiritual benefits received by Christians far outweigh what the world has to give. In verses 42–48, Jesus calls believers to be wise managers of all that God has entrusted to them. He has greater expectations of Christians than of unbelievers because He has revealed His will to us.

2. In Luke 12:16–21, the root problem was greed. In Matthew 25:1–13, the root problem was not being prepared. All knew the Bridegroom would return. None of the virgins knew when he would return. Some made provisions for a long wait and some did not. Matthew 7:26–27 is also about proper preparation. One's life must be anchored upon bedrock to

withstand the storms of life. The strong foundation is God's Word. See 2 Timothy 3:14–17.

3. Mary's focus was upon giving praise and honor to Jesus. She did not count the cost. Judas, on the other hand, was concerned about the cost of the perfume. He wanted the money for the disciple's treasury. In our personal use of money/wealth we can use it as did Judas, for only our own needs, or we can use it to honor and glorify God.

4. The Master was looking for faithfulness and good management. Two of the stewards fulfilled the expectations of the Master. The third steward was fearful. He did not trust the Master. The point is that God entrusts His property and business to us. He merely asks us to be faithful in our management of His property. The reward is the same for those who do great things or those who do not. The reward is out of Christ's grace. Revelation 2:10b " ... be faithful, even to the point of death, and I will give you the crown of life."

❖ Focusing on My Life

(About 10 minutes.)

Read the paragraph. Have the participants write a brief paragraph to express their understanding. Invite volunteers to share their paragraphs. Then read aloud the paragraph that follows. Discuss "A Christian's Four Basic Uses for Money." Then have the group discuss how we as Christians show our faithfulness and prudence in the management of the "talents" God has entrusted to us.

❖ To Close

(About 5 minutes.)

Sing or speak the hymn stanzas from "Take My Life, O Lord, Renew." Again ask members of the group to share concerns to be included in the closing prayer. Ask for volunteers to take the concerns to the Lord in prayer.

❖

❖ Focusing on the Week Ahead

(About 5 minutes.)

Encourage everyone to take time during the week to develop a written plan to manage the financial resources God has entrusted to them. Assist the group in understanding the worksheets that will be used for their budget planning. Obviously, the budget will not be shared with the group. Ask each person to pray for everyone in the group throughout the week.

Session 4

Showing Love
to One Another

❖ Focusing Our Sights

(About 2 minutes.)
Read aloud and discuss briefly the goals for this session.

❖ Focusing Our Attention

(About 5 minutes.)
Read the introductory paragraph of this section. Ask the group to react to what this paragraph says. Then discuss the three statements.

❖ Focusing on the Issue

(About 15 minutes.)
Have members of the group share their personal experiences. God works in our lives through many ways using different people to meet our needs. In turn, God will use us to help others in their time of need. Number 3 is a group exercise. Question 4 is meant to cause each participant to think of a specific person that they can help. Question 5 should help the group review the spiritual resources God provided to help them through their own crisis. Through this review the goal is to find the spiritual resources that will be most helpful to the person they have in mind.

❖ Focusing on God's Word

(About 15 minutes.)

Read the opening paragraph.

1. We are God's children because in His love He has chosen us for this high privilege. 1 John 3 and John 3 clearly tell us that we are who we are by God's action. Ask the group what picture comes to mind when they read in 1 John 3 that God has "lavished" His love on them. These two passages offer a wonderful opportunity to draw the class to the cross of Christ. Jesus urged all Christians to share the message of the cross. Read and discuss Acts 1:8 and Matthew 28:19. How do these passages apply to helping a person experiencing a financial crisis?

2. The key phrase for this discussion is found at the end of verse 10. The message is that a child of God will show love to his fellow human beings. See verses 11 and 16 where this message is repeated. How do these verses speak to the three statements in the "Focusing our Attention" section? Ask the participants what these verses mean to them in regards to their relationship with fellow human beings.

3. Read Luke 10:30–36. The Samaritan was not a Christian to the best of our knowledge. Why would Jesus have used the example of a Samaritan? The answer is that Jesus was using an extreme comparison to show the hypocrisy of the Jewish religious leaders. Discuss how Jesus would tell the parable today? Is the hypocrisy of the religious leaders found sometimes in Christians today?

4. Psalm 23 and John 10 once again focus our attention on the person and work of Jesus Christ. He is always the one to whom we turn in time of need because He alone is the Good Shepherd. As Jesus says in John 10, there are many pretenders. Only Jesus is faithful. We, through faith in Jesus, never have to doubt about the help we offer to others. He has promised to help. We can count on Him.

❖ Focusing on My Life

(About 7 minutes.)

Read and discuss Martin Luther's explanation to the
First Article of the Apostles' Creed. How does the First Article
address our needs, especially when we are experiencing a
financial crisis? Why would this article be important to share
with someone experiencing any kind of earthly crisis?

❖ To Close

(About 5 minutes.)

This may be the last time to pray for one another in this
setting. After speaking or singing the stanza from "Take My
Life, O Lord, Renew" invite everyone that is willing to con-
tribute to the closing prayer. Begin the prayer to start the
group concluding with the words "Lord, in your mercy." Ask
the group to respond with the words "Hear our prayer." Con-
tinue until everyone has had a chance to pray.

❖ Focusing on the Weeks Ahead

(About 5 minutes.)

Review with the group the importance of their use of the
means of grace through which the Holy Spirit works to
strengthen faith in Jesus. Encourage them to be diligent in
the study of God's Word. Encourage them to be regular in
worship, attendance at Holy Communion, and to participate
in fellowship with their brothers and sisters in Christ. Tell
them that you will pray for them and ask them to pray for
you.

To God Be the Glory!

❖

Real lives facing real frustrations need Connections to God and to one another.

CONNECTIONS

The **Connections** Bible study series helps take the concerns of your heart and turn them over to Jesus in worship, prayer, Bible study and discussion.

Connections uses a Gospel-centered message to build trust in God and to develop trusting and supportive relationships with one another, just as Christ intended.

Connections studies look at small portions of Scripture that really hit home, in areas where anxiety is often deepest.

For small groups or individual study, **Connections** uses God's Word to build relationships and bring peace to troubled hearts.

Ask for **Connections** *at your Christian bookstore*

H54821

CPH

3558 SOUTH JEFFERSON AVENUE
SAINT LOUIS MISSOURI 63118-3968